FOOTB

Other titles by Danny Byrne :-

Danny Gets to Grips with **Fishing**
Danny Gets to Grips with **Gardening**
Danny Gets to Grips with **Golf**
Danny Gets to Grips with **Horse & Pony Care**
Danny Gets to Grips with the **Motor Car**

Danny
GETS TO GRIPS WITH
FOOTBALL

DC Publishing Paperback

First Edition
Published in Great Britain 1996
DC Publishing
11 Bryanston Village
Blandford Forum
Dorset DT11 0PR

Made and printed in Great Britain

for
FOOTBALL FANS
EVERYWHERE

CONTENTS

FOREWORD

"Football is a National Game and within these entertaining pages everyone will recognise and chuckle at the one-liners and sayings that we all take for granted as professional footballers.

Danny's clever cartoon book is a must for every schoolboy embarking on a football course, to use as a light-hearted guide, together with the FA official manual.

The skilfully drawn illustrations will appeal to everyone, whether willing or unwilling participants of the sport as Danny has hilariously portrayed football situations at their funniest. All the cartoons will induce a smile even when your star player gets injured or your team lets you down.

This book is a reminder of how the game used to be played and should be played."

Lawrie McMenemy

It has been said that footballers
are born and not made.

Right from birth many parents have
great aspirations for their offspring.

Football tactics can be initiated
from an early age.

Young children cultivate incredible control skills.

Many children develop strong physical attributes such as power and pace.

We are all born with a certain balancing ability.

EQUIPMENT

For identification purposes, all members of the
same team wear the same coloured shirt.

The goalkeeper should wear something that
little more distinctive.

Shirts are allowed to bear the name of the
club's official sponsor.

Shin pads are vital to prevent serious injury.

Football boots with good studs are
beneficial for a firm grip.

PASSING.

Pinpoint your target for accurate passing.

A professional is blessed with poise.

Well-rehearsed passing always reaps rewards.

In team-play, retaining possession of the ball
is paramount.

Even in professional matches, it's amazing how
many passes are misdirected.

The bounce can vary from pitch to pitch.

To receive a pass it is essential to keep
your eye on the ball.

When closely marked, pass early to
avoid being caught in possession.

BALL CONTROL

To avoid injury, tense neck muscles
before heading the ball.

Trapping the ball with the foot can stop
the ball dead.

Relax chest muscles on impact
to deaden the ball.

Refrain from shouting advice to
your fellow players.

To kill a high ball, get underneath it.

SHOOTING

Accomplished players are able to bend
the ball with ease.

The overhead kick often
confuses the defence.

Whatever slips through the defence is often gathered by the goalie.

Selfishness has no place in modern football.

TACKLING

Concentration and controlled aggression are
needed for the sliding tackle.

Medics must be prepared for all eventualities.

Research weaknesses of the opposing team.

Reflex saves are a part of the goalie's defence.

HEADING

The head is a much used part of the anatomy
in the game of football.

Climbing on opponents shoulders is
considered foul-play.

Eyes should be focused on the ball
at all times.

Do not close your eyes, even at the
point of impact.

THE GOALKEEPER

There is nothing more reassuring than
a confident goalkeeper.

A competent goalkeeper should be able to
read the game from his goal area.

Goalkeeper's hands need very
special attention.

A good relaxed position is crucial for
the ace goalkeeper.

The goalkeeper is expected to shout
instructions to his team-mates.

There is nothing more spectacular than
the sight of a goalkeeper in full flight.

Today's goalie uses his feet as an
added line of defence.

Catching the ball with one hand is
extremely difficult.

A goalkeeper is responsible
for his entire goal area.

FOULS & MISCONDUCT

The Professional Foul

The law is enforced against players who intentionally commit offences.

Baiting the opposition is intimidatory and
will be penalized.

Time-wasting by the goalkeeper is not permitted.

Faking injury will not go unnoticed.

Go through the proper channels
when organising a re-match.

THE ROLE
of the
REFEREE

In controversial situations, the referee often consults the linesmen.

A good referee must be ready to diffuse
heated moments.

The referee is likely to address the teams
before play.

Not all fans question
the referee's credentials.

Knowing and understanding the rules
ensures progressive play.

The referee must remain
unbiased throughout the game.

THE MANAGER

Stress is evident in all managers.

The half-time pep talk.

A keen manager will go to great lengths to
enforce discipline before the big match.

The manager and his successful team join
together in post match celebrations.

TERMINOLOGY

BOOKING
The act of a referee following a serious
breach of the law.

THE DEFENSIVE WALL.
A wall created to prevent the opposing team
from scoring.

FLAT-FOOTED.
Leaving your opponent unbalanced and
feeling foolish.

SELLING A DUMMY.
An act to confuse a defender.

PENALTY SHOOT OUT
The goalkeeper's opportunity to shine.

MAN ON
Your opponent is closing in on you.

OVER THE TOP
A dangerous tackle.

TIGHT SITUATIONS.
When you are in close proximity
to your opponents.

DIVE IN
To react impulsively,
without composure.

FITNESS & TRAINING

Early fatigue causes the body to be unresponsive
to the brain's commands.

Star players undergo regular
stress and fitness checks.

Working closely with the coach
will heighten your reflexes.

Don't cheat during training sessions.
You will be letting the side down.

A fit team can strike fear
into the opposition.

To avoid serious injury,
warm up before playing.

Once you have reached peak fitness, you are able
to sustain 90 minutes of strenuous football.